# CRYPTO FUTURES TRADING FOR BEGINNERS

Secret Strategies to Earn Thousands of Dollars in the 2024 Crypto Bull Market

James Vega

# COPYRIGHT

All rights reserved. No part of this publication may be reproduced, distributed, or transmitted in any form or by any means, including photocopying, recording, or other electronic or mechanical methods, without the prior written permission of the publisher, except in the case of brief quotations embodied in critical reviews and certain other noncommercial uses permitted by copyright law.

Copyright © 2024, James Vega

**LEGAL NOTICE**

The information provided in this book is for educational and informational purposes only. It is not intended as financial or investment advice. The author and publisher of this book are not financial advisors, and readers should seek professional advice before making any financial decisions based on the content of this book. The author and publisher do not guarantee the accuracy, completeness, or reliability of the information presented, and shall not be held liable for any errors or omissions.

## DISCLAIMER

The content of this book is provided "as is" without any warranties of any kind, either express or implied. The author and publisher disclaim all warranties, including but not limited to the implied warranties of merchantability and fitness for a particular purpose. The author and publisher shall not be liable for any special, consequential, or incidental damages resulting from the use of the information contained in this book.

By reading this book, you agree to the terms and conditions outlined in the Copyright, Legal Notice, and Disclaimer. If you do not agree with these terms, you should not read or use the information provided in this book.

# BONUS

**PRACTICAL TUTORIAL GUIDE ON** :-

- How my Crypto Community member, Sam flipped his $100 to $10000 in One month using my untold Futures Trading secret strategies and How You too can use the strategy to make $10000 or more
- My crypto community Futures Trading challenge, Secret to my Crypto community 6 months Futures Trading challenge
- Buying Avax and sending to Trust wallet, how to buy coins using Poocoin
- How to flip your money to thousands of dollars using Swing trade
- How to transfer coin BNB to Trust wallet
- How to use Pancake swap and Poocoin

- How to spot, buy, and hold shitcoins and Gemcoins against the Bull Market Run and make millions of dollars from them.

To unlock this bonus, simply click on this link :- https://tinyurl.com/4MyCryptoSecrets

Or scan the below QR code.

**EXCLUSIVE CRYPTO FUTURES TRADING SIGNALS FOR COMPLETE 365 DAYS**

To unlock this bonus, simply click on this link :-

https://tinyurl.com/4CryptoProfitKit

Or scan the below QR code.

# TABLE OF CONTENT

COPYRIGHT
BONUS
TABLE OF CONTENT
PREFACE
INTRODUCTION
Chapter One
    Introduction to Crypto Futures Trading
        Understanding Crypto Futures and How They Operate
        Benefits, Risks, Margin, Leverage, and Risk Management
Chapter Two
    Getting Started with Crypto Futures
        Crypto Wallet Basics
Chapter Three
    Crypto Trading Futures Strategies
        Trend Following
        Range Trading
        Technical Indicators
        Fundamental Analysis
        Correlation Trading
        Rollover Concepts
Chapter Four
    Risk Management for Crypto Futures
        Importance of Risk Management
        Hedging Strategies

- Chapter Five
  - Avoiding Beginners Mistakes
    - Emphasizing Proper Risk Management Techniques
- Chapter Six
  - Tax Implications in Crypto Futures Trading
    - Understanding Tax Implications
    - Record-Keeping Practices
- Chapter Seven
  - Tax-Advantaged Trading and Recommended Exchanges
    - Tax-Advantaged Trading
    - Exchange Recommendations
- Chapter Eight
  - Market Psychology, Sentiments, and Market Cycles
    - Managing FOMO and Panic Selling
    - Understanding Market Sentiments
    - Bull vs. Bear Markets
    - How to Best Prepare For The Next Crypto Bull Run
- Chapter Nine
  - Futures Trading on Binance
    - Spot vs. Futures Trading
    - Liquidation
- Chapter Ten
  - Additional Learning Resources
    - Glossary of Key Terms
    - SHARE YOUR THOUGHTS

# PREFACE

Meet Sarah, a young investor who, by complete accident, found herself immersed in the world of cryptocurrency futures trading. As a result of her fascination with the prospect of huge profits and the exhilarating thrill that comes with trading, she decided to test the waters of this fresh and fascinating market. Without a doubt, she had no idea that this choice would alter the course of her life irrevocably.

Sarah began with a little investment and began learning the ropes of trading cryptocurrency futures via the use of Internet tools and tutorials. Her earnings continued to skyrocket as she built up her self-assurance and got more expertise, which led to her transactions becoming more strategic. Sarah was able to attain financial freedom and security beyond her wildest dreams by pursuing what began as a side pastime and quickly evolved into a full-time passion; this allowed her to realize her goals.

The tale of Sarah is a demonstration of the potential of trading cryptocurrency futures. It demonstrates how a willingness to take measured risks, together with devotion, education, and understanding of the market, can lead to success in this dynamic market. Those who are interested in becoming traders may draw motivation from her experience, which exemplifies the opportunities for expansion and financial success that are presented by trading in cryptocurrency futures.

# INTRODUCTION

In the fast-paced world of finance, the development of cryptocurrencies has transformed trading, presenting new possibilities and problems for investors. One of the most exciting parts of this digital transformation is the rise of crypto futures trading.

This book is a thorough guide aimed to help you navigate the difficult world of crypto futures, from comprehending the fundamentals to mastering advanced tactics. Whether you are a seasoned trader or a beginner in the world of cryptocurrencies, this book will give you the information and skills you need to thrive in this fascinating market.

# Chapter One

## Introduction to Crypto Futures Trading

## Understanding Crypto Futures and How They Operate

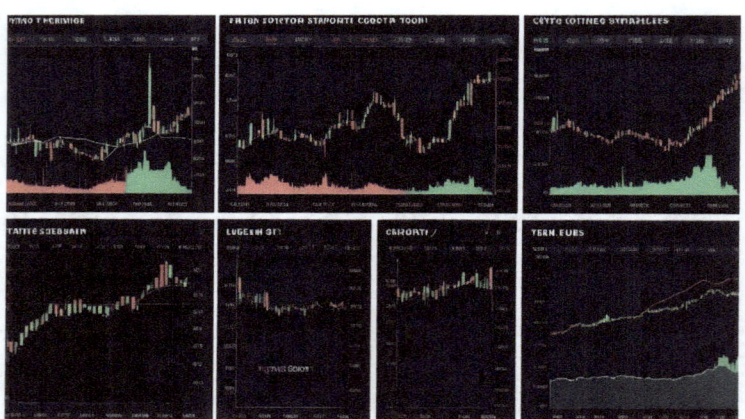

Crypto futures are derivative contracts that enable traders to bet on the future price of cryptocurrencies without actually holding the underlying assets. These contracts allow investors to benefit from both rising and declining markets, giving possibilities for hedging and speculating.

In basic words, when you trade crypto futures, you are effectively placing a bet on whether the price of a given cryptocurrency will climb or decrease by a certain date. This opportunity to benefit from market fluctuations in either direction sets crypto futures unique from typical spot trading, enabling more flexibility and possible rewards.

The functioning of crypto futures is founded on the notion of leverage, which enables traders to hold greater positions with a smaller quantity of cash. While leverage may enhance earnings, it also raises the danger of losses, making risk management a critical part of successful trading.

# Benefits, Risks, Margin, Leverage, and Risk Management

## Benefits of Crypto Futures Trading

- Liquidity: Crypto futures markets are very liquid, enabling traders to join and exit positions quickly and easily.
- 24/7 Trading: Unlike conventional markets, crypto futures may be traded 24 hours a day, seven days a week, offering sufficient profit potential.
- Diversification: Crypto futures allow investors to diversify their portfolios and protect against market volatility.
- Potential for High Returns: With leverage, traders may multiply their gains and capitalize on modest market changes.

## Risks of Crypto Futures Trading

- Volatility: The cryptocurrency market is notorious for its severe price changes, providing hazards for traders.
- Leverage Risk: While leverage may boost earnings, it also raises the possibility of severe losses.
- Market Manipulation: Due to the decentralized nature of cryptocurrencies, market manipulation is a problem in crypto futures trading.
- Regulatory Uncertainty: The regulatory framework for cryptocurrencies is continuously developing, adding an element of uncertainty to trade.

## Margin, Leverage, and Risk Management

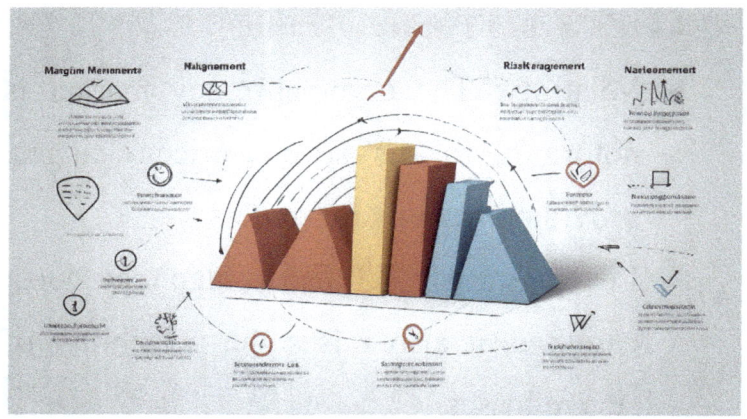

- Margin: Margin is the amount of capital necessary to start a position in a futures contract. It functions as a security deposit to cover future losses.
- Leverage: Leverage enables traders to hold greater positions with a lesser amount of cash. It multiplies both earnings and losses.
- Risk Management: Effective risk management is vital in crypto futures trading to safeguard money and reduce

losses. Strategies like stop-loss orders and position size may assist limit risks.

# Chapter Two

## Getting Started with Crypto Futures

Commencing your adventure into the realm of crypto futures trading demands a strong foundation and awareness of important concepts. In this chapter, we will dig into the basic procedures to get started with crypto futures, from picking a futures exchange to comprehending order types and contract details. By the end of this chapter, you will be armed with the knowledge and tools required to commence your trading career with confidence.

**Selecting a Futures Exchange**

Choosing the correct futures exchange is a key first step in your crypto futures trading adventure. Consider the following criteria while picking a platform:

- Reputation and Security: Opt for exchanges with a strong reputation and effective security measures to preserve your assets.
- Liquidity: Look for exchanges with substantial trading volumes to enable the smooth execution of deals.
- Supported Cryptocurrencies: Ensure that the exchange provides several

cryptocurrencies for trading to diversify your portfolio.
- Fees: Compare charge structures across multiple exchanges to reduce trading expenses.
- Regulation: Select exchanges that conform to regulatory norms to reduce risks.

Popular futures exchanges for crypto trading include Binance Futures, BitMEX, and Bybit, each providing distinct features and incentives for traders.

**Funding Accounts**

Once you have picked a futures exchange, the following step is to fund your trading account. Follow these procedures to fund your account securely:

- Create an Account: Register on the selected exchange and finish the verification procedure as necessary.
- Deposit monies: Transfer monies to your trading account using the available payment options.
- Manage Risk: Start with a cautious approach to risk management by dedicating a percentage of your funds to trading.

By filling your account wisely and managing risk properly, you set yourself up for success in the realm of crypto futures trading.

**Order Types**

Understanding various order types is key to completing trades effectively and optimizing profits. Common order types in crypto futures trading include:

- Market Order: A market order is executed at the current market price, assuring quick execution but perhaps at a different price than intended.
- Limit Order: A limit order enables you to select a precise price at which you wish to purchase or sell a contract. The deal will only be performed at the stated price or greater.
- Stop Order: A stop order becomes a market order after a particular price level is achieved, helping to minimize losses or lock in gains.
- Take-Profit Order: A take-profit order automatically cancels a trade whenever a defined profit threshold is achieved, helping to safeguard winnings.

Mastering these order types will help you to navigate the fast-paced world of crypto futures trading with accuracy and confidence.

**Contract Specifications**

Before getting into trading, educate yourself with contract details to make informed judgments. Key contract parameters to consider include:

- Contract Size: The size of a futures contract, which changes based on the cryptocurrency being traded.
- Expiration Date: The date on which a futures contract expires, after which it is settled.
- Leverage: The amount of leverage available for trading, which influences the margin necessary to initiate a trade.

- Tick Size: The minimal price movement permitted for a futures contract, determining profit and loss calculations.

Understanding these contract characteristics will help you understand the nuances of crypto futures trading and make educated trading choices.

## Crypto Wallet Basics

While trading on futures exchanges, it is vital to have a basic grasp of crypto wallets for storing and securing your digital assets. Consider the following sorts of wallets:

- Hot Wallets: Online wallets linked to the internet for quick trade yet subject to hacking.

- Cold Wallets: Offline wallets for holding cryptocurrency safely, away from internet risks.
- Hardware Wallets: Physical devices for keeping private keys offline, offering an additional degree of protection.

By familiarizing yourself with crypto wallet principles, you can secure your funds and trade with peace of mind in the risky world of crypto futures.

Getting started with crypto futures trading entails picking the correct exchange, financing accounts securely, learning order kinds, comprehending contract requirements, and grasping crypto wallet essentials. By following these critical steps and creating a solid foundation of knowledge, you are well-equipped to start your trading adventure with confidence and success.

# Chapter Three

## Crypto Trading Futures Strategies

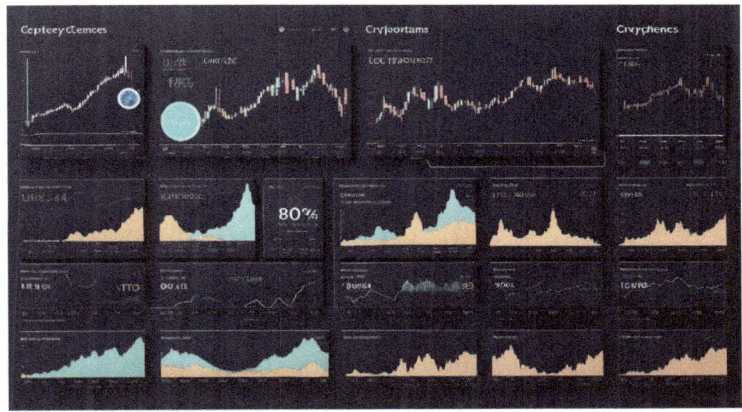

In the changing world of crypto futures trading, having a good plan is key to success. This chapter digs into several trading methods, from trend following to fundamental analysis, arming you with the knowledge and skills to navigate the complexity of the market with confidence.

## Trend Following

Trend following is a prominent method in crypto futures trading that includes recognizing and capitalizing on market movements. Key features of the trend following include:

- Identifying Trends: Use technical analysis methods such as moving averages and trendlines to find upward or downward trends in bitcoin prices.
- Entry and leave Points: Enter trades in the direction of the trend to maximize gains and leave positions when the trend shows symptoms of reversal.
- Risk Management: Implement stop-loss orders to safeguard money and manage risks efficiently while following trends.

By learning trend-following tactics, traders may ride the momentum of the market and capitalize on successful patterns in the realm of crypto futures.

## Range Trading

Range trading is a method that includes detecting price ranges within which a cryptocurrency is trading and taking advantage of price swings within that range. Key features of range trading include:

- Identifying Support and Resistance Levels: Use technical analysis to find critical support and resistance levels where price tends to vary.
- Buying Low, Selling High: Buy around support levels and sell near resistance levels to benefit from market moves within the range.
- Risk Management: Set stop-loss orders to reduce losses and adhere to stringent risk

management principles during range trading.

By understanding range trading tactics, traders may capitalize on price volatility within predetermined ranges and produce gains in sideways markets.

## Technical Indicators

Technical indicators play a significant role in assessing market movements and making educated trading choices in crypto futures. Common technical indications include:

- Moving Averages: Used to detect trends and probable entry or exit points based on moving average crossings.
- Relative Strength Index (RSI): Indicates overbought or oversold circumstances in the market, helping traders discover probable reversal points.

- Bollinger Bands: Volatility indicators that assist detect market extremes and probable trend reversals based on price volatility.

By adding technical indicators into their trading methods, traders may obtain significant insights into market movements and make educated choices based on data-driven research.

## Fundamental Analysis

Fundamental analysis entails determining the underlying worth of a cryptocurrency based on aspects like technology, acceptance, and market trends. Key areas of basic analysis include:

- Market News and Events: Stay updated on market news, regulatory changes, and technology improvements that might affect bitcoin values.

- Tokenomics: Evaluate the usefulness and scarcity of a coin to estimate its long-term worth and growth potential.
- Market Sentiment: Monitor market sentiment and investor activity to determine market trends and mood movements.

By integrating fundamental research with technical analysis, traders may construct a complete trading strategy that incorporates both market fundamentals and price fluctuations.

## Correlation Trading

Correlation trading includes examining the connection between multiple cryptocurrencies or assets to uncover trends and trading opportunities. Key features of correlation trading include:

- Correlation Coefficients: Use correlation coefficients to assess the link between various assets and find correlated or negatively correlated pairings.
- Diversification: Trade associated assets to hedge risk or diversify your portfolio to limit exposure to certain market swings.
- Risk Management: Implement adequate risk management measures while trading linked assets to safeguard money and reduce losses.

By understanding correlation trading, traders may harness the correlations between assets to make smart trading choices and improve their trading portfolios.

## Rollover Concepts

Rollover in crypto futures trading refers to the practice of extending or terminating a futures contract before its expiry date. Key rollover principles include:

- Expiration Dates: Understand the expiration dates of futures contracts and rollover holdings before expiry to avoid physical delivery.
- Rollover expenses: Consider rollover expenses, including funding rates and fees, while extending holdings to reduce trading costs.
- Roll Yield: Take advantage of roll yield by carefully rolling over holdings depending on market circumstances and price fluctuations.

By learning rollover ideas, traders may successfully manage their holdings and maximize their trading methods in the realm of crypto futures.

# Chapter Four

## Risk Management for Crypto Futures

In the turbulent world of crypto futures trading, proper risk management is vital to conserving money and increasing earnings. This chapter addresses the significance of risk management, position size, margin management, liquidations, margin calls, and hedging methods, providing you with the fundamental skills to negotiate the dangers involved in trading crypto futures.

## Importance of Risk Management

Risk management is the cornerstone of effective trading, helping traders preserve their cash and reduce losses. Key components of risk management include:

- Wealth Preservation: By managing risk efficiently, traders may conserve their wealth and ensure longevity in the market.
- Emotional Control: Implementing risk management tactics helps traders maintain emotional control and prevent hasty actions.
- Consistent Returns: Consistent risk management strategies contribute to steady returns over time, lessening the influence of market changes.

By emphasizing risk management in their trading technique, traders may limit possible losses and develop a strong basis for long-term success in crypto futures trading.

**Position Sizing**

Position sizing is a fundamental component of risk management, defining the amount of money allocated to each transaction based on risk tolerance and account size. Key concepts of position sizing include:

- Risk-Reward Ratio: Calculate the risk-reward ratio for each transaction to ensure that possible earnings exceed potential losses.
- proportion Risk per transaction: Determine the proportion of capital to risk on each transaction depending on risk tolerance and account size.
- Diversification: Spread risk across numerous transactions and assets to decrease exposure to specific market swings.

By understanding position size strategies, traders may optimize their risk-reward profile and manage capital efficiently in the tough environment of crypto futures trading.

**Margin Management**

Margin management is critical in crypto futures trading since it dictates the amount of leverage employed and the cash necessary to establish contracts. Key areas of margin management include:

- Initial Margin: The initial amount of money necessary to initiate a futures position, calculated by the exchange depending on leverage.
- Maintenance Margin: The minimal amount of capital necessary to keep a position open, below which liquidation may occur.
- Leverage: Use leverage carefully to enhance gains while controlling the risk of future losses.

By understanding margin management concepts, traders may optimize their use of leverage and margin to maximize trading opportunities while reducing risks.

## Liquidations and Margin Calls

Liquidations and margin calls are possible dangers in crypto futures trading, happening when a trader's account falls below the necessary margin amount. Key concerns for handling liquidations and margin calls include:

- Liquidation Price: The price at which a position is immediately terminated to avoid additional losses.
- Margin Calls: Notifications from the exchange to contribute additional cash to the account to fulfill margin requirements and prevent liquidation.
- Risk Alerts: Set risk alerts and stop-loss orders to monitor holdings and avert margin calls and liquidations.

By proactively managing liquidation risks and margin calls, traders may preserve their cash and prevent severe losses in the fast-moving world of crypto futures.

## Hedging Strategies

Hedging tactics are risk management approaches that include balancing possible losses in one position with profits in another. Common hedging tactics in crypto futures trading include:

- Long-Short Hedging: Simultaneously maintaining long and short positions to hedge against market volatility.
- Options Hedging: Using options contracts to guard against unfavorable market fluctuations and reduce possible losses.
- Cross-Asset Hedging: Hedging crypto futures contracts with assets from other markets to diversify risk exposure.

By adding hedging methods into their trading methodology, traders may limit risks, safeguard money, and traverse market volatility with confidence.

# Chapter Five

## Avoiding Beginners Mistakes

In the world of crypto futures trading, newcomers typically confront common traps that may limit their progress and lead to big losses. This chapter focuses on detecting and avoiding novice errors such as overtrading, revenge trading, lack of a strategy, and high leverage. Emphasizing good risk management approaches is vital to managing the hurdles of trading crypto futures efficiently and protecting wealth.

### Overtrading

Overtrading is a typical error among novices, defined by excessive trading activity motivated by emotions rather than a systematic approach. Key factors to prevent overtrading include:

- Quality Over Quantity: Focus on quality deals based on good analysis rather than numerous trades driven by impulse.
- Stick to Your strategy: Adhere to your trading strategy and avoid straying from it due to FOMO (Fear of Missing Out) or emotional responses.
- Patience and Discipline: Exercise patience and discipline in waiting for high-probability trading chances rather than pushing deals.

By identifying the pitfalls of overtrading and adopting a disciplined approach to trading, novices may avoid excessive risks and enhance their trading results.

## Revenge Trading

Revenge trading is a risky activity when traders strive to avenge losses by performing impulsive and high-risk bets. Strategies to prevent revenge trading include:

- Accepting Losses: Acknowledge and accept losses as part of trade, concentrating on learning from errors rather than pursuing rapid recovery.
- Emotional Control: Manage emotions and avoid making trade choices based on irritation, rage, or the need for retribution.
- Review and Learn: Analyze lost trades objectively to discover areas for development and change your trading style appropriately.

By building a mentality of resilience, learning from losses, and keeping emotional control, traders may stay clear of the harmful loop of vengeance trading.

**Lack of Plan**

Trading without a clear and well-defined strategy is a typical error that may lead to uneven outcomes and higher risk. Steps to prevent trading without a strategy include:

- Develop a Trading Plan: Create a detailed trading plan detailing your objectives, methods, risk management guidelines, and entry/exit criteria.
- Stick to Your strategy: Follow your trading strategy meticulously and avoid making hasty selections that depart from your stated boundaries.
- Regular assessment and Adjustment: Periodically assess and alter your trading strategy depending on performance, market circumstances, and developing objectives.

By building a systematic trading strategy and following it regularly, novices may better their decision-making process and raise their chances of success in crypto futures trading.

**Excessive Leverage**

Using excessive leverage is a dangerous strategy that may increase both gains and losses, leading to severe account depletion. Techniques to prevent high leverage include:

- Leverage Calculation: Calculate the right leverage based on your risk tolerance, account size, and trading style to minimize overexposure.
- Risk Management: Implement stringent risk management methods, including position size and stop-loss orders, to reduce the effect of leverage on your trades.

- Gradual raise: Start with smaller leverage levels and gradually raise as you develop expertise and confidence in handling leveraged investments.

By using care and discretion in leveraging positions, traders may limit risks associated with excessive leverage and safeguard their money from unneeded exposure.

## Emphasizing Proper Risk Management Techniques

Proper risk management tactics are necessary for novices to comprehend the complexity of crypto futures trading and preserve their investments. Key risk management concepts to stress include:

- Position Sizing: Determine the right position size based on risk tolerance,

account size, and trade structure to manage risk efficiently.
- Stop-Loss Orders: Set stop-loss orders to limit possible losses and safeguard money from large drawdowns.
- Diversification: Spread risk across numerous assets and transactions to decrease exposure to specific market swings and lower total risk.

By emphasizing basic risk management tactics, novices may develop a strong basis for effective trading, limit losses, and boost their prospects of long-term profitability in the hard world of crypto futures.

# Chapter Six

# Tax Implications in Crypto Futures Trading

Navigating the tax consequences of crypto futures trading is vital for traders to guarantee compliance with tax rules and improve their financial success. This section discusses the necessity of recognizing tax consequences, maintaining adequate record-keeping methods, and using tax-advantaged accounts to maximize tax efficiency in the arena of crypto futures trading.

## Understanding Tax Implications

Comprehending the tax consequences of crypto futures trading is vital for traders to prevent possible traps and maintain compliance with tax legislation. Key items to consider include:

- Capital Gains Tax: Profits from crypto futures trading are normally subject to capital gains tax, which varies depending on the holding term and tax location.
- Short-Term vs. Long-Term Profits: Different tax rates may apply to short-term profits (kept for less than a year) and long-term gains (owned for over a year).
- Tax Reporting: Traders are expected to declare their trading operations, profits, and losses correctly on their tax returns to meet tax requirements.

By understanding the tax consequences of crypto futures trading, traders may proactively minimize their tax obligations and maximize their financial plans.

## Record-Keeping Practices

Maintaining careful record-keeping techniques is vital for traders to monitor their trading activity, compute profits and losses properly, and simplify tax filing. Best practices for record-keeping include:

- Trade Logs: Keep full records of all deals, including entry and exit locations, trade dates, amounts, prices, and fees.
- Account Statements: Regularly check and preserve account statements from exchanges and platforms to monitor transaction history.
- Tax records: Organize tax-related records, such as 1099 forms or tax reporting statements, for correct tax filing.

By adopting comprehensive record-keeping standards, traders may speed up tax reporting processes, avoid mistakes, and preserve compliance with tax authorities.

**Tax-Advantaged Accounts**

Utilizing tax-advantaged accounts may provide considerable advantages to traders trying to improve their tax efficiency and maximize their after-tax earnings. Common tax-advantaged accounts for trading include:

- Individual Retirement Accounts (IRAs): Traditional and Roth IRAs offer tax benefits for retirement savings, enabling traders to grow their assets tax-deferred or tax-free.
- Health Savings Accounts (HSAs): HSAs provide tax advantages for medical bills,

allowing traders to save on healthcare costs and invest money tax-free.

- Education Savings Accounts (ESAs): Coverdell ESAs and 529 plans give tax benefits for education expenditures, letting traders save for educational requirements effectively.

By exploiting tax-advantaged accounts intelligently, traders may decrease their tax obligations, develop their assets more efficiently, and plan for future financial objectives with tax efficiency in mind.

# Chapter Seven

## Tax-Advantaged Trading and Recommended Exchanges

Exploring tax-advantaged trading tactics and leveraging suggested exchanges may dramatically improve a trader's tax burden and overall trading experience. This chapter goes into the notion of tax-advantaged trading, and ways to lower tax obligations, and includes suggestions for exchanges that provide advantageous circumstances for tax-efficient trading.

## Tax-Advantaged Trading

Tax-advantaged trading entails adopting methods and accounts that provide tax advantages to reduce tax obligations and

maximize after-tax earnings. Key components of tax-advantaged trading include:
- Tax-Deferred Growth: Leveraging accounts such as IRAs or 401(k)s to delay taxes on investment gains until withdrawal.
- Tax-Free Withdrawals: Utilizing Roth IRAs or HSAs to make tax-free withdrawals for eligible expenditures.
- Tax-Loss Harvesting: Offsetting profits with losses to minimize taxable income and capital gains tax liabilities.

**Reducing Tax Burden**

Reducing the tax burden associated with crypto futures trading demands careful preparation, smart decision-making, and adherence to tax-efficient techniques. Techniques to decrease tax costs include:

- Long-Term Investing: Holding holdings for over a year to qualify for reduced long-term capital gains tax rates.
- Tax-Efficient assets: Choosing assets with fewer tax consequences, such as index funds or tax-exempt bonds.
- Charitable Contributions: Donating valuable assets to charity to earn tax deductions and avoid capital gains taxes.

## Exchange Recommendations

Selecting the correct exchange for crypto futures trading is vital for optimizing trading conditions, accessing a large variety of assets, and benefiting from tax-efficient features. Recommended exchanges for tax-advantaged trading include:

- Kraken: Known for its extensive security measures, diversified asset offerings, and user-friendly interface, Kraken is a popular alternative for traders seeking a trustworthy and tax-efficient trading platform.

- Gemini: With a robust regulatory framework, transparent operations, and an emphasis on compliance, Gemini delivers a secure and tax-friendly environment for traders.
- Coinbase Pro: Offering extensive trading capabilities, a vast range of cryptocurrencies, and a flawless user experience, Coinbase Pro is a recommended exchange for traders searching for tax-efficient trading choices.

# Chapter Eight

## Market Psychology, Sentiments, and Market Cycles

Understanding market psychology, feelings, and market cycles is vital for traders to navigate the complexity of the crypto futures market efficiently. This section addresses handling FOMO and panic selling, strengthening trading abilities, reading market feelings, differentiating between bull and bear markets, and establishing lucrative trading methods to compete in the ever-evolving world of crypto futures trading.

### Managing FOMO and Panic Selling

Managing Fear of Missing Out (FOMO) and panic selling is vital for sustaining emotional discipline and making reasonable trading choices. Strategies to manage FOMO and panic selling include:

- Setting Clear Objectives: Define your trading objectives and techniques in advance to prevent impulsive actions prompted by FOMO.
- Implementing Stop-Loss Orders: Use stop-loss orders to safeguard your holdings and avoid panic selling during market volatility.
- Staying updated: Stay updated about market trends, news, and events to make educated judgments and avoid falling into emotional responses.

By handling FOMO and panic selling efficiently, traders may maintain a disciplined approach to trading, decrease emotional biases, and boost their overall performance in the market.

**Enhancing Trading Skills**

Enhancing trading abilities is vital for traders to react to changing market circumstances, enhance decision-making processes, and maximize trading results. Techniques to strengthen trading abilities include:

- Continuous Learning: Stay informed on market trends, technical analysis tools, and trading methods to increase your knowledge and abilities.
- Practice and Experience: Engage in simulated trading or paper trading to practice methods, try new ideas, and earn vital experience.
- Seeking mentoring: Learn from expert traders, seek mentoring, and join trading forums to obtain insights and viewpoints from seasoned professionals.

By consistently polishing their trading abilities, traders may develop their tactics, make educated judgments, and enhance their expertise in navigating the complexity of the crypto futures market.

## Understanding Market Sentiments

Understanding market attitudes is vital for evaluating price movements, spotting patterns, and making educated trading choices. Key factors of market emotions include:

- Greed and Fear: Recognize the influence of greed and fear on market behavior, since they typically cause price swings and market cycles.
- Contrarian Indicators: Monitor contrarian indicators, such as sentiment surveys or positioning data, to measure market mood and prospective trend reversals.

- Market Psychology: Study market psychology, investor behavior, and emotional biases to forecast market changes and profit on trading opportunities.

Understanding market attitudes and psychology will help traders to get significant insights into market dynamics, predict price moves, and adapt their methods appropriately for more effective trading results.

## Bull vs. Bear Markets

Distinguishing between bull and bear markets is vital for adjusting trading techniques to existing market circumstances and maximizing performance. Characteristics of bull and bear markets include:

- Bull Market: Characterized by increasing prices, optimism, and investor confidence, bull markets give possibilities for long holdings and profit-taking.
- Bear Market: Marked by decreasing prices, pessimism, and investor uncertainty, bear markets demand care, risk management, and possible short-selling methods.

# How to Best Prepare For The Next Crypto Bull Run

It is Q1 of the year already , and many people are looking forward to their financial freedom and enjoying their life.

It's also the time of year when crypto fans, entrepreneurs, and experts start to predict how they believe the crypto market will perform next year, and if the next bull run will finally come after a protracted bear market in 2023.

This conjecture tends to focus on how well Bitcoin (BTC) and Ethereum (ETH) will do, but also covers the performance of various altcoins, and if there will be viable blockchain acceptance for particular chains. For the most part, there is a lot of confidence behind these projections, and in some instances, extraordinarily positive outlooks for the price of BTC.

But here lies the dilemma.
Although it's wonderful to be positive, the fact is that no one can forecast how the market will be in 2024, or when the next crypto bull market will be upon us. What you can do, however, is to plan for the possibility of a fresh crypto bull run,

and there are recommendations on how to best prepare for one. Before we do, it is vital to first look at what makes a crypto bull run.

**What is a Crypto Bull Run**

The conventional understanding of a cryptocurrency bull run is when there is a 'sustained gain' in price across a considerable number of crypto assets. Furthermore, investor confidence is generally strong during this time, which in turn leads to greater purchasing activity; further pushing up prices.

So whereas many of us may assume that we know what a crypto bull run is, contrary to common assumption, what makes a bull run is subject to interpretation, and there are multiple measures that different individuals use (individually or collectively) to identify one.

Below are some frequent indicators:

This is not an endorsement. There is no infallible approach for forecasting the future success of the crypto market, any signal should still be treated as speculative.

- Price rise: The most popular sign utilized by most crypto fans is whether or not there is a substantial and persistent rise in the price of cryptocurrency.

In terms of the time range, this is subjective and down to each individual, although a bull market is commonly measured across weeks or months.

- Market Cap rise: Another frequent bull run indication cited by analysts is if there is a considerable rise in the entire market capitalization of the crypto ecosystem. This takes into consideration the overall worth of all cryptocurrencies, and not simply the price of individual coins.

- Trading Volume: A signal that tends to follow upward price movements is a jump in trading volume, which if extended, would lead some to interpret this to be evidence of a bull market; indicating heightened investor interest and market involvement.

- Media Coverage/Sentiment: Some less technical and seasoned crypto aficionados may at times dip into an assortment of various media sources to see if the sector has broken out of crypto winter, or whether the beginnings of a bull run might be occurring. This may be happy news reports, declarations that particular blockchains have been embraced by mainstream corporations, or very bullish market analyses by crypto influencers; just to mention a few. Please note that while many people use these as indicators, there is no evidence to imply that any of them are valid indicators.

- Blockchain acceptance: In the view of blockchain purists, a bull run might be heavily contingent upon underlying technical improvements, and an increasing acceptance of cryptocurrencies and its underlying technology.

This is more of a basic analytical approach.

- Institutional Investment: Last but not least, big institutional investments into the cryptocurrency market might imply a degree of maturity and stability that some analysts may perceive as the commencement of a bull run or the extension of one.

Suffice it to say, whilst most people would view a bull market as a sustained increase in price across a significant number of cryptocurrencies, the indicators above show that not everything is black and white and that many different variables could potentially indicate that a bull run might be happening.

## When is the Next Crypto Bull Run?

Now the issue that every crypto fan wants the answer to - when is the next crypto bull run?

Whilst it would be simple to offer an arbitrary Bitcoin price forecast for next year or provide a subjective view on when the larger market would have continuous growth, the truth of the matter is that it is hard to make reliable predictions for bull and bear markets.

However, this hasn't prevented some crypto influencers and media sites from professing to know when the next bull run will come and providing very bullish price forecasts.

But as indicated above, considering how there is no foolproof formula for forecasting future market movement, these forecasts are not only untrustworthy but highly reckless; seeing how people spend money depending upon what they say.

A more rational approach is to accept that while there is no way to predict what the future holds for the crypto sector, there are some signs that might perhaps allow individuals to foresee a prospective bull market.

Below are two forthcoming events that some people feel might be early markers of a likely bull run in 2024. This is not an endorsement. There is no infallible approach for forecasting the future success of the crypto market, any signal should still be treated as speculative.

## Bitcoin ETF

Historically, the larger crypto market has tended to prosper or suffer based on Bitcoin's success. For this reason, happenings around BTC have likely been the most widely monitored subject by speculators who are seeking possible bull market indications. One keenly observed development has been reports of a Bitcoin ETF potentially obtaining regulatory clearance. According to Galaxy's Michael Novogratz, the reason why this is a promising sign for some investors is because a regulated spot bitcoin exchange-traded fund might result in billions of dollars coming into Bitcoin ETFs each year. Novogratz has now followed up by claiming that a regulated Bitcoin ETF might result in BTC hitting its all-time high again ($65,000 in November 2021).

## Bitcoin Halving

Another much-followed development has been the forthcoming Bitcoin halving event. A Bitcoin halving occurs every four years, it is when the cryptocurrency halves its mining incentives. This reduces the pace at which new Bitcoins are generated, and as a consequence of this, some individuals feel that this new scarcity might lead to a rise in the price of BTC owing to a stronger demand.

This event is carefully observed by investors and fans alike, and most feel that this may have a huge influence on the larger cryptocurrency market.

Tips For Preparing for The Next Bull Market
Because there is no infallible method to pinpoint when a bull run will happen (and to what degree), presenting speculative forecasts is more likely to inflict more damage than genuine help, hence making this a very irresponsible thing to do. What can be supplied, however, is advice on how to effectively prepare for the inevitability of a bull market.

Below are 4 recommendations that might assist you in preparing for the next bull market:

This is not an endorsement. There is no infallible approach for forecasting the future success of the crypto market, any signal should still be treated as speculative.

**Historical Research**

The first thing you can do is to study prior crypto bull runs. Although there is no evidence to imply that this is a legitimate signal, some feel this exercise might perhaps give some insights into patterns and timings that could indicate that a bull run is coming. This may involve looking at items that caused (or corresponded with) earlier bull runs, how long they lasted, and how different cryptocurrencies reacted. You may also balance up prior global economic and technological, and see if this is connected at all with previous bull runs.

**Fundamental Analysis**

Another item that some individuals may utilize to prepare for a prospective market boom is fundamental analysis.

This entails assessing cryptocurrencies based on their intrinsic worth, which involves examining at a project's whitepaper, tokenomics, underlying technology, and collaborations. Looking at these elements, and understanding how they build value for a cryptocurrency might signal great growth potential; and hence, possible choices for a large bull run.

## Exchange/Platform Research

It may be beneficial to research suitable exchanges and trading platforms. This is to guarantee that things move smoothly and effectively during a possible bull run. Things to consider include evaluating a platform's transaction costs, convenience of usage, security features, liquidity, and the number of cryptocurrencies that are offered.

## Tax Planning

Last but not least, since cryptocurrencies are subject to taxes in many countries, it is vital to plan for the prospect of having to pay tax on any profits realized during a bull run.

Crypto tax may be highly difficult and time intensive, thus it is essential to contact a tax specialist who has experience with crypto taxes before any prospective bull run. Moreover, make sure to maintain accurate records of your transactions and asset kinds, since doing this close to the end of the tax year may be highly time-consuming and unpleasant.

**Profit Strategies**

Developing effective trading methods entails finding entry and exit opportunities, managing risk, and responding to changing market circumstances. Profit methods to examine include:

- Trend Following: Capitalize on market trends by taking positions in the direction of the trend and leaving before the trend reversals.
- Range Trading: Trade within price ranges by purchasing at support levels and selling

at resistance levels to benefit from price swings.
- Counter-Trend Trading: Identify possible trend reversals and trade against the existing trend to capture short-term price fluctuations.

# Chapter Nine

## Futures Trading on Binance

Futures trading on Binance brings up a world of opportunity for traders to participate in complex trading techniques, leverage their holdings, and traverse the unpredictable crypto market with accuracy. This section analyzes the contrasts between spot and futures trading, the mechanics of long and short positions, the function of leverage, liquidation risks, order types, and hedge mode, and gives general trading recommendations to optimize your trading experience on Binance Futures.

## Spot vs. Futures Trading

Spot trading includes purchasing or selling assets for immediate delivery at the current market price, whereas futures trading involves entering into contracts to purchase or sell assets at a fixed price on a future date. Key distinctions between spot and futures trading include:

- Spot Trading: Immediate settlement, direct ownership of assets, and exposure to current market pricing.
- Futures Trading: Contractual agreements, leverage to magnify holdings, and the chance to benefit from both rising and declining markets.

By knowing the differences between spot and futures trading, traders may exploit the benefits of each to enhance their trading strategy on Binance.

## Long and Short Positions

In futures trading, traders may take long positions to benefit from price gains or short ones to profit from price drops. Key characteristics of long and short positions include:

- Long Position: Buying futures contracts with the anticipation of a price increase, seeking to sell at a higher price for profit.
- Short Position: Selling futures contracts with the expectation of price depreciation, seeking to purchase back at a lower price to conclude the position and make profits.

By understanding long and short positions, traders may profit on market moves, hedge risks, and diversify their trading tactics efficiently on Binance Futures.

## Leverage

Leverage enables traders to handle bigger positions with a smaller amount of cash, increasing both gains and losses. Important factors related to leverage in futures trading include:

- Leverage Ratio: Determining the leverage ratio to limit position size and exposure to market swings.
- Risk Management: Implementing effective risk management measures to limit the impact of leverage on trading results.

Margin needs Understanding margin needs, maintenance margins, and the effects of leverage on account balances.

By applying leverage carefully, traders may maximize their trading potential, optimize capital efficiency, and handle the complexity of futures trading on Binance with confidence.

## Liquidation

Liquidation happens when a trader's position is automatically liquidated by the exchange to avoid additional losses owing to inadequate margin. Key factors involving liquidation risks include:

- Liquidation Price: The price at which a position is liquidated to safeguard the exchange and the dealer from additional losses.
- Margin Calls: Notifications from the exchange to contribute additional cash to fulfill margin requirements and prevent liquidation.

- Risk Alerts: Setting risk alerts and stop-loss orders to monitor holdings and avert liquidation occurrences.

## Order Types

Different order types enable traders to make transactions based on unique criteria and preferences. Common order types on Binance Futures include:

- Market Orders: Executed at the current market price, giving quick execution but no price guarantee.
- Limit Orders: Set at a predetermined price level, allowing price control but no certainty of execution.
- Stop-Limit Orders: Activated when a certain price is achieved, transforming into a limit order to restrict execution price.

By employing numerous order types strategically, traders may optimize their entry and exit locations, manage risk effectively, and boost their trading accuracy on Binance Futures.

**Hedge Mode**

Hedge mode allows traders to open long and short contracts simultaneously to balance risks and safeguard their portfolios from unfavorable market fluctuations. Key features of hedge mode include:

- Risk Mitigation: Hedging against prospective losses by balancing long and short positions to balance market exposure.
- Portfolio Diversification: Managing risk by diversifying trading techniques and holdings to decrease overall portfolio volatility.

- Market Flexibility: Adapting to changing market circumstances and uncertainty by adopting hedging measures to safeguard money.

**General Trading Tips**
- Risk Management: Prioritize risk management procedures, including position sizing, stop-loss orders, and diversification to safeguard money.
- Continuous Learning: Stay updated about market trends, trading tactics, and platform features to better your trading abilities and expertise.
- Emotional Discipline: Maintain emotional control, prevent impulsive actions, and adhere to your trading strategy to obtain consistent outcomes.

By adopting these basic trading recommendations into your trading practice, you may enhance your decision-making processes, optimize your trading results, and boost your performance on Binance Futures.

# Chapter Ten

## Additional Learning Resources

Expanding your knowledge and abilities in the field of crypto futures trading demands access to reputable and dependable instructional materials. This chapter analyzes suggested blogs, YouTube channels, online courses, and books to expand your grasp of trading methods, market analysis, and essential ideas in the realm of crypto futures.

Additionally, a glossary of important phrases is offered to aid your knowledge and promote a full grasp of the terminology used in crypto futures trading.

**Trusted Blogs**
- CoinDesk: A major source of cryptocurrency news, analysis, and insights, CoinDesk's blog gives vital information on market trends, regulatory developments, and trading methods.
- CryptoSlate: Known for its in-depth research, reviews, and analysis of the crypto business, CryptoSlate's blog offers a plethora of information for traders and investors.
- The Block: With an emphasis on blockchain technology, cryptocurrencies, and market trends, The Block's blog delivers professional comments, market research, and industry updates for traders seeking important insights.

Reading reliable blogs in the crypto field help traders remain updated, obtain important viewpoints, and make educated judgments in their trading activity.

**YouTube Channels**
- Crypto Jebb: Known for technical analysis, market updates, and instructional videos, Crypto Jebb's YouTube channel provides useful insights for traders trying to develop their trading abilities.
- Coin Bureau: Providing in-depth reviews, lessons, and market analysis, Coin Bureau's YouTube channel is a go-to resource for traders seeking thorough information on cryptocurrencies and trading tactics.
- DataDash: Focused on market research, trading advice, and industry news,

DataDash's YouTube channel delivers a combination of technical analysis and fundamental insights for traders of all levels.

Subscribing to trustworthy YouTube channels in the crypto realm, traders may receive instructional information, remain current on market movements, and enhance their trading knowledge and abilities.

**Online Courses**

- Coursera: Offering courses on blockchain technology, cryptocurrency trading, and financial markets, Coursera offers a choice of online courses for traders wishing to enhance their expertise in the crypto business.

- Udemy: Known for its extensive course offerings, Udemy includes bitcoin trading classes, technical analysis lessons, and risk management tactics for traders wishing to develop their abilities.
- Binance Academy: Binance's teaching portal, Binance Academy, provides free courses on blockchain, cryptocurrencies, and trading tactics, giving significant tools for traders wishing to increase their expertise.

Enrolling in online courses from reliable platforms, traders may access organized learning materials, develop new skills, and remain ahead of the curve in the quickly expanding field of crypto futures trading.

## Recommended Books

- "Trading in the Zone" by Mark Douglas: A classic in trading psychology, this book covers the attitude and emotional discipline essential for effective trading.
- "Technical Analysis of the Financial Markets" by John J. Murphy: A thorough approach to technical analysis, this book covers chart patterns, indicators, and trading methods for traders of all levels.
- "Cryptoassets: The Innovative Investor's Guide to Bitcoin and Beyond" by Chris Burniske and Jack Tatar: Offering insights into the world of cryptocurrencies and blockchain technology, this book is a helpful resource for understanding the crypto market.

## Glossary of Key Terms

- Leverage: The use of borrowed capital to enhance trading positions and possible rewards.
- Margin: The collateral necessary to initiate and sustain leveraged positions in futures trading.
- Liquidation: The process of liquidating a trade to avoid future losses owing to inadequate margin.
- Stop-Loss Order: An order issued to automatically sell or purchase an asset at a predefined price to minimize losses or lock in gains.
- Hedging: A risk management method including establishing offsetting positions to hedge against unfavorable market moves.

- Bull Market: A market characterized by increasing prices and investor confidence.
- Bear Market: A market typified by decreasing prices and investor pessimism.
- Market Sentiment: The entire attitude or mood of market participants towards an item or market.
- Order Book: A real-time collection of purchase and sell orders for an asset, offering insight into market depth and liquidity.
- Risk Management: The process of recognizing, analyzing, and managing risks to preserve capital and maximize trade results.

## SHARE YOUR THOUGHTS

Your feedback matters! If this book has enriched your understanding of crypto futures trading and empowered your trading journey, we would greatly appreciate your positive review. Share your insights, experiences, and how this book has impacted your trading strategies. Your review can inspire and guide fellow traders on their path to success. Leave your mark and help others discover the value within these pages. Thank you for being part of our trading community!

Share your Futures Trading passion! Leave a review on www.amazon.com

We can't wait to see your creativity come to life!

www.ingramcontent.com/pod-product-compliance
Lightning Source LLC
Chambersburg PA
CBHW050326230526
45471CB00005B/2371